EXPOSING MYSELF

STANLEY CHRISTOPHER

This book is dedicated to the individuals who have consistently supported me in the driven development of my writing career.

Also by Stanley Christopher

A Sought After Love: A Collection of Sonnets

Acknowledgements

In appreciation of those who have gone and those who remain, helping to shape the ongoing story of my life.

Contents

Exposing Myself

I'm coming up here
opening up here and
spilling bits of my
soul spilling them
whole out on these
yellowing wet pages
spilling in ruined
stages and jazzy
hot plundered days
crippled and healed
ages pruned from
the strange fruit
lying splayed open
and rotting washed
and re-washed in
the roaring troubled
waters and warming
Pina coladas and in
the fogginess of
crumpled distress as
my heart rages and
screams and the fat
lady sings and creams
over the toes of my
shoes and under the

souls of her mules
while engaging herself
in harmonious blues in
the midst of fantasy
vacations at the
heart of wet dreams
crushed and destroyed
by surreptitious opinions
designed to void the
life out of my reach
constantly stretching
for my freedom of
choice my liberation
of voice my right to
free speech my not so
rosy or sweet external
fired beats mirroring
those internal hidden
desires heat right here
on these yellowing
pages in blatantly open
shamelessly filled up
with love hope and a
shattering of a wounded
and slow healing soul of
stiffening resistance I
yes am exposing myself

Part I: Back to Black

Stanley Christopher

Did You Open the Door

Did you open the door for her?
Tell me my eyes didn't see true
You were raised better than that
Is that the best that you can do?

Did you not pull out her chair?
Another chance missed to impress
You could have made up for the door
With that special skill of finesse

Why didn't you hold on to her hand
As you strolled up the busy avenue
If you'd of slipped your arm into
hers she would have felt brand new

Kiss her fingers, pinch her cheeks
Whisper sweet nothings in her ears
Let your love for her sink in deep
Build her faith, dissipate her fears

Understand this one thing my son
For your manhood looms at hand
It's your job as a dutiful Father to
Teach her what to expect in a man

Stanley Christopher

Getting Past The Booty

Damn Ol' Skool, check out that Ass,
I could run that to the alley and
wax it down real fast
So many hot booties out here tonight
with some as fine as apple pie
and you know I gotta have a bite

Young blood, let me say, I'm kind'a
long in my day, so I got a little
something under my belt
And all the love, joy and pain that
you'll ever feel, believe me I've
already felt

There are no lessons in life of worth
from death back to birth, 'less you
take them in as you should
I have a few words to impart, please
take them to heart, 'cause this is
for your own good

Sometimes she's like a wind-up toy
and you're the one with your finger
poised on the button
When you twist her emotions, when she
had no notion, she'll snap and change
all of a sudden

Exposing Myself

Treat her wrong and you can be sure
she'll rise up raging like a fierce
blowing tempest
Treat her right and pump up her worth
and she'll be calm as she becomes
your strong Empress

See this is the sweetest part of the
whole thing, you'll experience once you
get past the booty
Man up and learn, then you can earn
the reward of getting to know her inner
natural beauty

Tenderly treat her soft and gentle,
stroke her cerebral like a delicate
blooming flower
In this brand new behavior you'll
come to discover the seed of your
infinite power

For to handle a fragile sparkling gem
takes sensitivity of emotional stroke
oh so very rare
To strike balance you must be strong
to smooth the rougher edges you'll find
here and there

*To do this you must develop a focus
that views her as the highest her that
she can be
Then support her and nudge her, never
begrudge her, and her third eye will
open to see*

*Do this and the two of you will become
one, you'll have your place in the sun
care free
You won't be alone when this union's
full grown, 'cause your hearts and souls
will agree*

*Now that I've imparted these words unto
you, I hope they ease some potential
future strife
Go out into the world using your head and
heart, be free as a lark, and enjoy a good,
long happy life*

My Woman so Black

My Woman so Black
her name should be
jazzy bluesy mellow
juicy slick slack

An onyxized stack
filled with life's joy
makes my lips smack
quality fitted woman
no cheap brick a brac
An astute intellect
as sharp as a tack
Golden tan molasses
warm caramel cream snack
My ebony dynamo helps
keep me on track by
giving me sweet love
so I'm giving it back

Yeaaaaaaaaaa yea
My Woman so Black
her name should be
jazzy bluesy mellow
juicy slick slack

To My Queen Of Queens

You held me deep inside
nurtured me as I grew
In you I did reside
'til you birthed me new

You rocked me in your arms
suckled me at your breast
Kept me from the worlds harms
And always did your best

You nourished my body
stirred my fertile brain
You taught, be somebody
Not bound by lock or chain

Through harsh times, hard and lean
you carried the great load
You taught me by being
strong through every episode

Went to work, paid the bills
You did it all alone
Kept the house, cooked my meals
All these things, on your own

10

Exposing Myself

When I was down low sick
You never left my side
As solid as a brick
In you I could confide

For the full duration
The time in which I grew
You were my foundation
Always stood proud and true

In consideration
For all that you went through
With appreciation
My Queen Mother, I love you

He Is My...

He lays there all balled up
gently snoring, I approach
the foot of the bed, I know
I will linger here a moment,
an eternity and my eyes well
with bitter tears, I am so
afraid, so, afraid for him

A quickly maturing lion
balancing on a trembling
precipice teetering on the
whim of a society that would
most gladly extinguish his
shining, daring fire in a snap
as in snuffing out a match
"Poof!"

How do I steel his armor to
encounter and confront their
little deceitful ways and
dastardly tricks? Yet I have
survived the poachers traps,
cut down by his abstracted
fire stick, I have arisen,
mane in tact, full black

12

flowing rivers in the sun
And I shine, I shine, I grow
more mature daily, I thrive
and bask healthy in the light

I look to my first born, my
Man child, a tear wells my eye,
I no longer fear, My heart
beats a thundering drum in my
broad chest, Any fear, wispy
smoke in the breeze reaching
out to the sun set to the cool
twilight horizon, of dying day.

He will be fine. He has risen
fathered his own pride, sired
his own continuance of a bold
and mighty strain. He is mine
He is ferocious, He is fearless
He is compassionate. What more
could I ask of my or any God
He is my advancing heart, he
is my ascending spirit, He is
the jubilant celebration of
the reason for my own existence
He is my Lion King

Untitled

In the midst of this madness
In this vastness of churning
universe
As the insanity of the chaos
is unfurled
The progress of human is turned
to reverse

Echoes bind us into what used
to be
as march to forward grinds to
a halt
And the end of this time allows
us to see
Everyone are to blame it is not
one man's fault

So we must become as universal
under cloak
To remedy the sickness of heart
felt dis ease
To render it useless ending time
this slave yoke
Seek an unveiling of soul healing
cosmic breeze

Starting Place

Hello My Sister and Brother
from the same Ancient mother
We've been drilled, trampled
to believe that we are other

They taught you we never took
this lands opportunities while
never voicing how hard they've
worked to keep us on our knees
begging for Justice and fair
Equalities while they lied to
make us all mortal enemies

Now it is time to become united
disseminate the vital truths
That we all originate from the
same strong roots
Not according to colors of
different degrees but reaching
much deeper in our humanities and
destroying the lies and mythes of
so-called race and going beyond
hue of skin, age and cast while
learning to respect the common
seed of all of our past

Stanley Christopher

When it's all said and done we
should acknowledge through grace
We all of us began in the same
starting place

The Dark Shadow That Covers

I strolled the fields at equinox
I trod upon the ashes and grain
and wondered how the darkness of
it all could return again and again

I washed my hands at the water's edge
among the scaly shackles and shells
and wondered how the blood could come
flooding back filling well upon empty well

I bowed my head in lowly prayer last night
away from the prying eyes of all man and
asked the center of all that be to lift
the dark shadow that now covers the land

I Am Black Man

I am Black man
I am Father to all
In my veins flows the
life blood of all mankind

In my eyes rests the atrocities
and accomplishments of the world
And I am angered and ashamed at the
actions of my children unto themselves

It was never my intent that you all be
like greed crazed animals, as you have become
All that I have channeled to you has been tainted
by the poisonous acts you have undertaken against
one and all others

Into my ears echoes the myriad screams and
cries of anguish and torment you create
as you betray the legacy of love and strength
that I handed down to you to assure you a
bright, happy existence for generations to come

Exposing Myself

Into my nostrils flow the foul stench of death and
decay rising from the horror of your warring ways
You barter like whores with their tricks to gain
surreptitious control over what is not yours to
control

And in my throat you have left a briny bitter taste
gagging my hope and faith in you as worthy heirs to
the
legacy of joy and wonderment I built in my
undertaking
to assure you a long existence of true peace and
tranquility

I am Black Man
I am Father to all
And I am angered and ashamed
At the actions of my children unto themselves

I am Black Man
I am Father to all
And I am angered and ashamed
At the actions of my children unto themselves

I Am

I am the holy breath of the
Great Mother that squatted
in the fertile lush gorges
along Olduvai to give birth
to the all of mankind while
bearing the scars of past
violations and abuses still
fertile spewing forth rich
black oils exotic spices
minerals and sparkling gems

I am the mantle of the
sons of the Sun who
scooped up the wide wind
blown sands of the Sahara
to erect monumental city
states laid in the eternal
shadows of the pyramids

I am the steel heart that
pumps the life blood of
the showers that feed the
luxurious jungle lands and
dries to arid dust storms
to form the red loins of
the wide spread Serengeti

Exposing Myself

I am the brilliant colored
fabric that paints the broad
variety of flavors the base
the construction of a proud
majestic race called hue men
in joyous spiritual ceremony
to celebrate the glory of
my all magnificent existence

I am the holy breath of the
Great Mother that squatted
in the fertile lush gorges
along Oldivi to give birth
to the all of mankind while
bearing the scars of past
violations and abuses still
fertile spewing forth rich
black oils exotic spices
minerals and sparkling gems

I Am Afrika

I Cry For...

I Cry
I cry for myself and my loss
I cry for the 150 million of myself
I cry at the pain of that darkness
I cry at the coldness of that crossing
I cry for the numbness that lingers still

God I feel that I might die of it all
This passage has been such a collective alone
The chill of that dank drink is still to the bone
And on that salty air I hear my freedom call

I howl
I wail for the ongoing cost
I howl for the darkness that's left
I wail at the sting of deaths' cold kiss
I howl at the ending of the dark ones bossing
I wail because it has become my skill

And the passage continues until his fall
Though the heart be icy, it's flesh not stone
And the end is at hand for he stands alone
And clings destruction like a warm winter squall

Truth Ever Present

Now present are the sores
Obvious as I peer out over
the fields
Fields of starvation and hunger
The gash of oppression gapes
before us
Revealed are the faces
faces of the myriad soldiers
the soldiers of the people
the soldiers are the people

Now present are the cries
cries that were like whispers
whispers in the dead night
Rattles of quiet ghost chains
chains that bound the myriad
the myriad in the death fields
fields of course cotton boles
fields of the harsh plantations
fields of endless oppression

Now present are the chants
the chants made of prayers
Prayers upon the dying fields
Dying fields of holy prayers

Stanley Christopher

holy prayers of resistence
resistance in fields of cotton
cotton fields of battle cries
cries for freedom's release
freedom from oppression

Now present are the truths
truths that churn and grow
grow more everyday evident

Wars

There are rumors more are coming
As the dirges go on humming
And the total of the summing
Is they'll never go away

Dark angel we hear you creeping
Your excitement we feel leaping
Deaths cool slumber we'll be sleeping
As life's essence skews astray

Draped in each new days sunshine
Upon the bloody landscapes shrine
Where vultures hungry come to dine
Here no more shall children play

Battle standards on high flying
Courageous men go right on dying
And their deaths still leave us crying
As bright futures turn to clay

But in deep faith we keep praying
That Gods' light yet will be staying
The icy hands that do the slaying
And halt their endless foray

I'm Writing This Poem (For Every Brother)

I'm writing this poem for every Brother
That has come to the realization that
Everyone attempts in their own little
Sanctimonious fashion to destroy a bit
Of his dignity, his pride, his very worth.

I'm writing this poem for every Brother
That sees through the constant bullshit
That is laid out daily like a crisp
New burial shroud in the gross attempt
To swaddle up his mind / his spirit and
Cast him / millstone about his neck /
Hands lashed behind his back / into the
Raging seas of failure and disappointment.

I'm writing this poem for every Brother
that ever received a threatening letter
From the state because he doesn't filter
The support money through their grubby
little mitts, for which he is labeled /
Lazy / cheap / and no account

I'm writing this poem for every Brother
That has had to rock himself to sleep

Exposing Myself

Under the banner of degenerate animal
Even as he witnesses the rape, the pillage,
the very brutalization of all his Mothers /
All his Sisters / all his Daughters

I'm writing this poem for every Brother
That seems to fall short of being able to
Provide what little girls have been raised
To expect from their man even while the
whole of society denies him equal access
To the pursuit thereof

I'm writing this poem for every Brother
That is stalled out of the main stream
Because he doesn't possess the adequate
Experience to get employment because he
Hasn't had adequate employment in which
To gain the necessary experience

I'm writing this poem for every Brother
That remains in the streets and homeless
Because no one will rent to him because
He has no presentable rental history
Because no one would rent to him because
He is homeless

I'm writing this poem for every Brother
That has had his window and windshield
Smashed/ tires flattened/ wires pulled/
Gas tank sugared/ clothes cut up or burned/

Stanley Christopher

House broken into/ property destroyed/
Pockets rifled/ address book and privacy
invaded/ pictures returned, burned or
Ripped up, by his so called wife/ woman/
Female/ lover/ Girlfriend/ ex/ lady/ boo/
Or fatal attraction

I'm writing this poem for every Brother
That has ever been escorted from his home/
Snatched from the streets/ nightclub/ car/
public or private functions/ etc., and
forced by those deemed to be in authority
To spend even one solitary night in one of
Those concrete and steel cages in the name
Of justice and all that is right

I'm writing this poem for every Brother
That has puzzled over why it seems to
Be considered alright and fair game to
Effect just about any destructive act
That one might care to commit upon or
against his person

I'm writing this poem for every Brother
That has had enough of this crazy life
And spirit draining bull shit and I'm
Writing this poem to wish a hail and
hearty Fuck You from every Brother that/
In the face of all these diverse stones
Of daily oppression and confusion/ has

Exposing Myself

Come to the realization that in the
Final analysis/ his shear refusal to
Remain lying face down/ the very act
Of steady and steadfastly getting back
Up/ the decision to finally and forever
Stop being the weak victim/ is now and
Evermore truly his only genuine salvation

I'm writing this poem for every Brother

Invention of a Dog

They say we are all Dogs
and in those words they
erase any innocence we
ever had but I remember
when I was a little pup

I still remember how she
took my member and she
put it into her mouth and
when I began to cry she
shut me up in the closet

She repeated that until
I decided that I was more
afraid of the dark in the
closet than the darkness
lurking inside her mouth

Why Don't I Drive?

I failed the written
drivers test twice
and when I finally
passed it the state
took my license for
back child support
on my two grown
daughters who live
with me

What's it Really Like

What's it really like
being Black
Do you really feel the
white man crawling up
your back
Does it really feel
like life won't give
you any slack
Do you feel you give
your everything never
receiving one thing
back and in the game
of finance you can't
get up on your stack
without doing some
crazy thing like
going out there to
deal crack

Or maybe you are more
grounded and all the
weight on your back
is your own stone
and you carry it and

deal with it because
you know that you're
grown
your higher power is
always with you so
you never feel alone
and you view your
situation as a ruler
on a throne and all
that may once have
burdened you has all
raised up and gone

What's it really like
being Black and always
trying to remain on
track along with
dealing with all the
flack
Well I guess it all
depends on where your
mind and spirit are at

Selfish Me

Picked your cotton
made your beds
Slaved in the belly
of the beast
body breaking mills
and factories

was I supposed to
kiss your ring
lick your boot
strings
for oppressing me
and perpetuating my
slavery

And you frown deep
in your brow
wondering how
I could in all my
ungrateful audacity
rebelliously
disagree
with your life long
plan for my kind
and me

shiftless lazy peons
unskilled laborers
working your fields
nurturing your kids
cleaning your homes
rocking your heads
sun up 'til past down
true peace never found

How dare I dare to
want one solitary
moment for myself
how disgustingly
vicious and damn
greedy of me

downright staggering
that I even have the
nerve to see
a life without you
depending on me
how horrible how rude
and despicably selfish
could I really desire
to be

They Do Not Play

I am an artist/poet
painting masterpieces
of life's stone vapors
manipulating the words
and thus so the language
into panaceas of bluesy
sorrows and sparkling
glitters of happiness
yet I know our tomorrows
can't always be bliss
borne on communication
tinted and flavored by
ghetto life human strife
Friday night fish fries
and party 'til we dies
and we struggle in a
constant state of late
while closing our eyes
otherwise as a disguise
feeding ourselves lies
refusing to see our fate
as we try to relate to
the story that we let
somebody else narrate

36

Exposing Myself

and fall for the bright
glittery bait and play
the game they orchestrate

Existing in a shadow place
labeled "no niggers allowed"
No Black niggers and no
Puertorriqueño niggers no
Vietnamese niggers and
no greaser Mexican niggers
no Jewish niggers and no
Native American niggers
no Cuban niggers and no
dusty ass Haitian niggers and
No not even no White niggers

Show us your "I Give Up" card
and we'll pretend you're not
really niggers until we
don't need you anymore
don't need you to
mop the floor no more or
mind the store no more
keep you until we can
find a cheaper whore
keep you for as long as
you just stay down in that
can't get out this hole/playing
that old can't come up role

This is all predicated on the
non-negotiable condition that
you sell your very soul and
beware we don't take no lip
we don't and we won't give up
on this vise-like bulldog grip
made iron clad by our whip
whether that be cold physical
or be that old mental trip

Because we're always seeking
out and finding and importing
new niggers and by the time
they figure it all out it's
too late they've sealed their
own fate and if they protest
they become enemies of the
state regulated by our ever
constantly renovated and
updated "no nigger allowed"
open ended falsely befriended
unwritten policy mandated and
re-blended and up ended because
you know times change and laws
must too in order to allow us
to continue to do what we do
to you and all the other hip
niggers it's true

Exposing Myself

So buckle it on down and keep
your nose to the old grind stone
because we have the ability to
leave you powder dry to the bone
and remember wherever you may go
we've raised haters and snitches
to hold you steady in tow and
keep their eyes on our riches so
watch out what you do and watch
close what you say because we
run this dirty low down system
in every conceivable way holding
it down and running the block all
the time we keep it up tight with
strapped glocks drawn and cocked
and we absolutely and unequivocally
always keep fingers on our triggers
because you can put this on yo' mama
we still eradicate & eliminate niggers
A Word to the wise it would do no good
to pray all night and on trough the day
'cause We're cold blooded monkey devils
and you know... We Do Not Play

You Did That Didn't You
(Tribal Chant)

You did that didn't you
Stole my women and kids
You did that didn't you
Beat knots about my head
You did that didn't you
Bound me down with chain
You did that didn't you
Tried to entrap my brain
You did that didn't you
Strived to keep me down
You did that didn't you
Penned me to the ground
You did that didn't you
Kept my face in the dirt
You did that didn't you
Always hit where it hurt
You did that didn't you
Locked me up in the pen
You did that didn't you
and then did it again
You did that didn't you
Forced to labor for free
You did that didn't you

And put the blame on me
You did that didn't you
Hung me up with a rope
You did that didn't you
Took my life for a joke
You did that didn't you
Lashed me like a mongrel
You did that didn't you
Branded me the scoundrel
You did that didn't you
Ripped my body apart
You did that didn't you
Aiming to slay my heart
You did that didn't you
Didn't want me to read
You did that didn't you
Said I couldn't succeed
You did that didn't you
Set my body to flame
You did that didn't you
Said twas in Jesus name
You did that didn't you
Told me not to believe
You did that didn't you
Said Jesus ain't for me
You did that didn't you
The root of my forbid
You did that didn't you
Oh you know that you did

But then there came this
that you couldn't expect
That all of your negative
I would totally reject

And all the evil stuff
you know that you done
only grew me up strong
to reach up for the One

Bet you didn't know all
along you were doing that...

Now did You?

Welcome To You

You went around that corner
Skulking a Burglar on the
prowl you marched around
that lane full of your own
self-authority chest swollen
up like a Thief and for a
time that's what you were
you were a Stalker then
you were an Assaulter

You Assaulted that child
because you thought he was
going to be an easy mark
you thought he would be
something soft and you
Accosted him physically
and you found you were
getting more than you had
bargained for you had bit
off more than you were
ever prepared to chew up

In the thin shadows of
the night surprisingly
yes suddenly that child

*was Beating Your Ass and
in that moment in that
instant you became the
worst kind of Thief you
knew how to be because
you Coward that you are
Slithered through the dark
of night and Viciously*

STOLE THAT BABY'S LIFE

*Then you and the Slimy
Heartless Animals the
Powers That Be began to
spin it began to make it
look like it was about a*

BLACK AND WHITE THING

and you aren't even

WHITE

*What you and those Powers
That Be are are Dirty Low
Down Calculating Vermin -
Parasites that Prey upon
those who are powerless*

Thieves that you are you
turned around and like a
million times before you

STOLE JUSTICE

But it wasn't about hue
the fact is you

A GROWN ASS MAN

MURDERED A BABY

Not a BLACK BABY but an

AMERICAN BABY

And in that he was ours

ALL AMERICANS

So when you toss and turn
in the night understand
this madness that is slow
creeping overtaking you
is your own doing - your
own creation - you chose
this in the blink of an
eye and this Hell that
daily you must live with
is you and you can't get
away from you and that

public smile you wear
cannot belie the life
sentence you must serve

Welcome to your very own
self-chosen interment

WELCOME TO YOU

Part II: Spirit and Space

Stanley Christopher

A Brand New Ending

Dear Son
I apologize for not
being there
I just didn't know how
but I do still care
Didn't even know how to
be there for your ride
because though of age
I was still a kid inside
My dad wasn't there
for me
but that's no excuse
because I didn't even
realize how much I
needed him in my youth
So I just made it up
as I went along
I was fierce even mean
but I didn't know how
to be strong
I talked down to your
mom because I felt
she was greedy and
even if she was this
weakness was inside me

Stanley Christopher

So I took to the streets
to seek out my man self
only managed to get more
lost and endangered my
health
I got shot and got stabbed
as my growing self was
smothered and all I really
learned was to do the same
to my brothers
Blind I stalked by-ways
and alleys on the verge
of insanity in this dark
search for my elusive
masculinity
Still without instruction
it grew into macho with
no boundaries and took a
while to see we are not
born with masculinity
It's something we earn
No woman can give it to
you
No matter how filled her
heart with love that's true
It's a man thing to learn
and can take a lifetime to
get it
some never do and live lives

that are stunted

But we are both blessed by
GOD who sent you back to me
because back in your life is
where I should be
and although we can't start
from the very beginning we
can pick up right here and
start a brand new ending

Daddy

I remember him hefting me
light as a feather to land
gentle upon his shoulder
strolling me about the
neighborhood Momma locked
arm in arm by his side at
the age of two I already
knew that out of a magic
place pride and I have
walked this fair journey
him always lifting me up

Dear Gabrielle

Hey my Sweet Chocolate Dream
I remember the night yo mama
gave birth to you there was
me sitting in that brightly
lit hallway looking into that
room full of new born babies
and you the only one who was
not crying because you knew
as I knew that Daddy was there
loving you like he would the
rest of our lives and beyond

Faith

Across this grey and
desolate plain
The dimming gloom of
fall grows here
And from a lifetime
of shameless stain
is drawn from sorrow
a tear

iridescent memories
turned tarnish dull
draped in a clinging
cloak of fear
whispered warnings
cause the lull
As winter's dead
draws near

The scent of dis ease
lingers on
Twisting the roots at
sanities poles
And though withered
to the very bone
The bright new light
still unfolds

Fantasy Island - A Sonnet

I'd like to move way far away from here
To a far off distant paradise place
Somewhere I can be full of fresh new cheer
With not one single old familiar face

An island with a tranquil sandy beach
And exhilarating fresh ocean air
Where I can place myself way out of reach
Taking my whole life to be free of care

Waving Coconut palms would line the shore
I'd lay around in the warm sun all day
And I'd never long for anything more
On that paradise isle I'd always stay

Yes that would be the sweetest life for me
A far off land a long way out to sea

Hope

Hope is an empty
self-filled thing
to cushion the hurt
and ease the pain
yet in the end
they still remain
a shattered song
with no refrain
She props me up
to carry on
still desire
lingers strong

I Am Idealistic Youth

*I spark the light that
reveals the path to the
what will be
I am the hand of present
that reaches into future
to change what has been
the world and thus also
all of man kind
I am your strength, power
and spirit carrying on
forever*

I am idealistic youth

I Want to Be Me

I want to be me and
I don't want how
somebody treated me
determining for me
who I want to be
I want to decide
how and who I want to

be my own self for me

Into The Silence

Where do you go when

there's no place to go

and all about you

most hands are all in

What do you do when

you know that you know

that it's time for some

new thing to begin

How do you feel when

you know that you're real

but the world is on

a fake ego trip

Do you stand up and

shout, make a big deal

or hold it all in

while biting your lip

Stanley Christopher

Do you seek outside

for distractions sake

To escape the gone

mad din of the crowd

Do you go confide

about what to take

so the craziness

doesn't scream to loud

There's a quiet

place to mellow out

come face to face with

yourself, have no doubt

Rest calm, simple grace

from your dis-ease route

'cause to go with out

is to go without

Turn inward to see

There's no distraction

Exposing Myself

You must examine

yourself from within

Your soul must come free

reach satisfaction

Allow your spirit

to purge all the sin

Into the silence

is where you need go

shining more brilliant

than fresh golden rod

In to alliance

move into the flow

because this is the

place where you see GOD

Lesson Learned

There comes a point where you find
you've grown to be very polite

It can be such a hard and cold feeling
to give up your possessive ways

So you're polite... and it takes
tremendous effort

but effort to do any other thing...
otherwise...
Well there is just no otherwise

So you're polite and you swim around
in this grey-green ooze that sparkles
and bubbles
And you pray for salvation, for
metamorphosis

And suddenly you can feel... maybe
sense it
And the ooze is clearing... you shimmer
in it's light
Not blinding light, not crystal clear...
but you know

Exposing Myself

Though you can't see it... the better path
has already been cleared for the long
continued journey
Myriad are the twisted and turned, pulled
and pinched like salt water taffy...

Oh the bittersweet joy of new growth
Another lesson is being learned

Righteous Enough

It's difficult and awfully painful to be real
I can hardly stand the hurt of letting people
be themselves
Striving to help them be themselves
I have already been all too selfish in my
giving of myself
I have further tarnished the temple and
strained against change
Yet how can I be responsible unto anyone
else
if I am not responsible unto mine self
And this... this peeling away of layers and
layers
of shirking my responsibilities of human
hood...
This painful, dull light... this spreading of
fresh
new found petals are rebirth
The tears are but the bittersweet dew
upon the new growth
And these lie... any first steps are stumbling
and unsure
but as these lessons are learned reality of
true self is manifested

64

And true self is righteous enough for all
whom one meets that are righteous
in themselves

Sunday Morning: Daddy Dressing

Handsome mountain of a man
stands in the steamy essence
of soap and shampoo shaving
thick cloudy lather away
draping his stone strong jet
countenance in crisp white
freshly starched and folded
extracted out of clear like
glass laundry package shiny
bright like brand new tucked
smooth into belted sharply
creased suit pants held
straight loose and swaying
like a players waist to
ankles covering of this man
prayer - silk like nylon hose
almost sparkly in the dawning
morning light slipping into
spit shined shoes reflecting
the stunning black of a holy
night - matching stud tack
anchoring noosed loose adorning
his neck and down his chest and

links locking stiff cuffs in
place - suit coat pressed as
smooth as a gentleman of leisure
going to check his corner
stables confusing sisters of
morning service - how can a
gentleman of such swag and
charisma be serving up anything
for God - slid back stocking
cap silky as black satin like
rippling waves secured by a
healthy spread of Murry's balm
and cooling splash of Brute or
maybe Old Spice Father's day
gifts worn like the oil of Jesus
He is the Hymn Houser so filled
with gospel songs he is rumored
to be where they all had been
originally stored - he once
taking a Christmas card
transforming it into a carol

And this every Sunday ritual
the center of activity of the
entire household in unison
with the Royal Leader - Daddy

The Light Binds Us

The light binds us together
Even in the darkness it seeps in
To wash us in it's warm softness
Revealing the secrets that hide
Rooting out the mysteries
Exposing the all of it to our eyes
And we in shame finger each other
And pray that the light misses us

It won't... it can't
It is what adheres us, wraps us
Swaddling, moaning in the manger
Exposed to the shining stars
We are the beast that in the
beginning bayed at the moon
Howling in our loneliness until
We learned to finger each other

And hide from the light
And now we moan hot
Hot sighs, hot lies, hot thighs
Yes moan, moan in the dark
Whimpering joyous fear tossing
Turning, flipping, flailing,
Bound even in the very darkness...
By the light

This Connection

I.

I sit in the Sun
outside the shop
waiting to be served
The other side of the avenue
shut down and torn up
making way for city's
brand new light rail train
On my side the cars creep
to a wet stop for the light
She sits in her white jag
head bobbing lipping words
the volume is minimal
lyrics almost subliminal
she smiles in her enjoyment
and waves
I nod my head/acknowledgment
and smile inside at the
spirit of our connection
this connection of it all
of all humankind/beyond
A sense of serenity comes
envelopes my heart/soul

II.

It has been raining
the cars/tiny splashes at
the edge of the curb
brings me back from my
spiritual nap
An older woman approaches
she nimbly jumps back
avoiding
threatening car spray
recovers/hesitates
looks at me and smiles
I smile/nod acknowledging
her light fright/relief

Beautiful day isn't it
I agree
We talk of the harsh
Winter/it has just passed
we enjoy even more the
warming Sun as we
remember
Again I am engulfed by the
cosmic magic/connection
beyond race beyond class
even beyond hate/death
she strolled into the shop/store

III.

The workshop manager/worker
comes out to say/your turn
I follow him in/he is jealous of
my time spent in the Sun
I smile/He mentions the long
frigid Winter
worst in fifteen years
together we give thanks
for the onslaught of this
rainy yet warm new season
And I am washed once again
by the beyond/of all differences
this condition
I smile a little prayer
deep inside in an all consuming
thankfulness

This connection
is different from all other
connections/ yet it spans to
encompass the entire
spectrum of connection
This connection channeled
through the energy of
the universe/beyond

Stanley Christopher

I casually realize I left my
little snack bag of
jelly beans/cashews at home
Wishing I had them along with
to offer a few/in celebration
of this connection

Traveling From A Distance

What are we doing in this verbal trembling?
And where should we be in the light of it all?
Is this a real exorcism of the temple?
or just a rehashing of a ghostly recall
A true purging of that tiny part of the soul

What are we seeking in this guttural rumbling?
This the price of the bet we made at the post?
Or are we just clearing the musty air?
Butterflies shedding ancient ageless cocoons
Reborn to bask in the black sun renewed

As dizzy euphoric episodes breeze in and out
Is this our spiritual destiny, our fate?
Irony supreme in its passing wake of joy
And can this peaceful buzz sustain the light?
Or is wisdom its own empty reward?

Does the growing process feed upon itself?
Replenish the void to the state of overflow?
Is this new-wroughtness exuberant enough?
Sufficient in its own elusive fortitude
I bear the cross of the future for the urge
at the root of my soul

True to Self

"Squeeze the very juice out of life or
the wasted fruit will rot at your feet"
     Nappy Smooth

Life left me screaming
wondering where it was
leading
I watched it fleeing
proceeding
to some far off rewarding
place
and I watched as my face
made the mirror dull
in the glare of
incandescent light
all the gloom rushing out
dark as night

Whispers came gentle
stiff urging
leave this place
leave this flat race

Exposing Myself

Become the product of
your own faith
Seek and see what ye
might find
zone out your up tight
diminishing light mind
grab her by her wild
hairy mane
and never let go again
ride her until every
ounce
of your cosmic energy
is drained
never refrain
from splitting it wide
open
and gorging 'til
appetite is sated and
nothing remains

Bask in the sun
wallow in the rainbow
take a single mother
to lunch
take in a show
and show yourself to be
what you actually know

yourself to be
a good reason
to grow full in your
season
of celebration
free of strife
and capitulation

It is the only sane and
reasonable thing to do
be true to being true
to yourself
in being you

Young Man How Song

Young man how blind are we
Young man how blind are we
We so blind we scarce can see
Young man that's how blind we be

Young man how lost are we
Young man how lost are we
We so lost we still ain't free
Young man that's how lost we be

Young man how far we roam
Young man how far we roam
Gone so far can't find our home
Young man that's how far we roam

Young man how cursed we be
Young man how cursed we be
We so cursed we need God's mercy
Young man that's how cursed we be

Young man how we find our way
Young man how we find our way
We must bend on our knees to pray
Young man that's how we find our way

Stanley Christopher

Young man how we win our race
Young man how we win our race
We wash in the blood of our savior's grace
Young man that's how we win our race

Part III: Word Cruises

Stanley Christopher

Dave

I rescued you once from
a slamming screen door
released by our angry
sister and you eagerly
trying to follow stepped
into the tiny abyss
between door and step over

My arm shattering glass
in my moving forward the
horror that gripped my
heart had you gotten cut
but you were just fine
and I was alright too

Daddy took me for stitches
and a chocolate malted
and you lay in your crib
fast asleep when I came
back home
My most intimate memory
of us interacting as one

Day Dream

Today came at me
like a twisted whirl
wind lacing in and
about the sinews and
the twine weaving an
emotional pantomime
of clear crystalline
patina dropped in
cascading rushes and
weedy skin flushes
and like a light
breeze the whole
brushes my spirit
and wisps me on away
leaving cosmic soul
echoes like a cool
spray from the rough
water's edge rocking
me swaying me like
a jumper on a windy
thousand foot ledge
as I fall out of bed
and I scream I soon
realize it was only
a very strange dream

Home

I wandered away a time ago
Got distracted, led astray
But In time I grew a flow
Keeping the wolves at bay

Something was missing though
Always at the edge of my mind
It took time but now I know
What out here I can't find

Home Sweet Home

As you read these

words I am entering

you

I am entering through

your eyes, your

finger tips, entering

through your brain

slipping in across

your lips

breath me in

can you sense me

entering your nostrils

a veiled odorless

vapor pouring misty

slow through your head

Exposing Myself

across your tongue

down your throat

tickling lightly at

your esophagus

billowing your lungs

quaking, oozing down

into your belly

drifting there as a

ship in full blown

sail

I came to stay

this no meager visit

This is an inner

body experience

I am now a part of

you

can't you feel me

all snuggled, nestled

Stanley Christopher

flexing in your

muscles, coursing

through your veins

swelling your every

cell, your every

membrane

Thank you for

allowing a small

part of me to

take up this

residency deep

within thee

feels like

home sweet home

Jazz Fest in the Park

Sparkling lights flicker
and spin strung in time
weave and twine hung
suspended in rhyme they
climb like stairs to the
inner mind to the rafters
illuminating and vibrating
the hustling bustling crowd
of smiling faces like
Christmas in the summertime
heads bobbing to the waning
and rising bounce of bass a
guitar pinching and lean
mean yet to clean to sting
pierces out a scalding
twang permeating ear and
brain as driving repeat
of lightening and rumble
beat drummed like peaked
mountains climbed in hot
icy heat too cool to
review better than brand
new and too chilly for
crackers while vibes hip

tumble almost stumble and
slip to trickle drops that
drip in oceans of sound
sweet delicious profound
from high above to way deep
down underground washing
away the grit and grime of
the day leaving one to shake
one's head and say...

Now that's some smooooth
Shiiiit

Pieces I Return To

There are pieces I keep going back to
They all have something special to say
There are lessons I've learned from a few
They're positioned in a certain way

Wordtonic plates they slide and shift
As they transform with every new read
And some of them give my soul a lift
While others still make my ears bleed

New adventures lay within these words
Of verbal roller coaster rides
Filled with potions and lexiconic birds
Taking flight to where magic resides

Into this concert I listen deep
For the silence between every note
Because I don't ever want to sleep
On the messages these sages wrote

That's why I keep going back again
To drink at these cool verbal springs
It's my own fluidity I'm trying to maintain
I'm inspired when their succulence sings

Stanley Christopher

There are pieces I keep going back to
They all have something special to say
There are lessons I've learned from a few
They're positioned in a certain way

Poetry To Me

Stretching the boundaries
of language with abstract
twists and turns barely
controlled skittering and
gleaning along the edge
testing the limits of
the precipice teasing the
bottomless abyss flinging
catapulting the matter of
time and space contrasts
taunting the ridge along
terminals of exploration
and discovery enhancing
the melodious fluid flow

Poetry

Built a boundless parameter
of iambic pentameter to meter
and structure said same
when it comes to this poetry
I'm kind'a like floetry except
I'm a lion of natty dark mane

seeded and nurtured in verb and noun rows,
picked, washed, and packaged tight verbal flows,
of adverbs and pronouns, a myriad words,
feeling the energy of the love your soul heard

promiscuous brackets, quotes splayed out in ink
from the pen of a romantic who with love is in sync
laced with carnal knowledge and magical creams,
pressed through soul scorching, sacred orgasmic
dreams,
from the heart of this ocean emulsifying, twining,
streams
comes the alchemistic adhesive binding us in these
love seams

Exposing Myself

Language, slithering, sliding, flipping capsizing,
comes slipping right in hypnotizing,
deep into those orifices mesmerizing,
teasing and tickling those hot temperatures rising

Trembling balancing on the edge
like dangling on the end of a string
and abstractly erotic cookie does sing
and each happily drained landing is
like being reborn in spring

Remembering My Mother Nature

My birthplace, a dwindling industrialized frontier
overwhelmed by steel mills and cement plant,
sitting on the edge of beautiful Lake Michigan.
Sandy beach so ill-treated, decimated by broken
glass, charred wood and rusty nails, left over from
bon fires of irresponsibility and you could not
walk those debris infested sands barefooted. The
water turned a sickened motley green spewing
forth on regular basis, wave upon wave of dead
silver fish filling the air with the odor of death.
We almost managed to kill Mother Nature there.

Then the mills shut down no longer puffing and
belching their multi colored poisons into the air
giving us spectacular pink and purple sunsets.
The weeds and vines returned to engulf
the abandoned train tracks leaving the
cargo and box cars with the appearance
of floating on a wall of tall green grasses
The cement plant went silent leaving heaps
of garbage out back where kids hunted
for the treasure of R.C. Cola tops win
10 cents, 25 cents forever in search of the
ever elusive non-existent win 10 dollar cap

Exposing Myself

*Then the builders moved to the opposite
border a wonderful wetland we called the
prairies, our classroom in the outdoors
red winged black birds, sneaky brown
cowbirds laying their eggs in other birds
nests, reeds and cat tails planted in muddy
wet soupy marsh filled with tad poles, tiny
frogs, garter snakes and slow poke snails*

*They built a research lab there, they built
a library there too, they drained away dear
Mother Nature, good-bye, they bid her die
Now the lab is closed and the city board
argues about closing the last two city
libraries, but no one speaks of restoring
the magical wetland of my ago spent youth
Maybe they will put up a new parking lot
They're really good at stuff like that*

Saint Paul Nocturne

In this place the twilight river

glistens moonlight in the

ripples washes right through

me and dulled winter's glow

evidences the sparkling blue

of fallen snow enveloping the

whole of my being less being

In this place my sleepy head

spirit rambles 'cross bridges to

coffee house to theater to cafe

chapel bells chime soundtrack

to bold tender heart of a saint

as shadowed sculpture gardens

dance in the hue of night's light

In this place I come returning

96

Exposing Myself

as to home and grasp to my

breast the charming homespun

nice born of this place home of

ice castles and winter carnivals

celebrating ecliptic solstice as

sirens scream from the distance

Comes the Winter (2014)

Enters the charge ripping into/through
cities that are twins inherent alone
the beast released from hiatus long
comatose status returning on angry
wings/winds specter of past-post
destruction/murder punishing/torturing
those who dare to attempt forgetting
straining/bowing backs changing stats
stranding the adventurous who defy to
grind on forth in forging icy mythos
pitched in rotting disdained/refrain
the maddening bombardment/barraged
frozen/abandon locking down in howling
sounds doorways/pathways/highways
school days quietly falling ravishing
testing the spirits of those who have
here/there proclaimed undying loyalty
and claim this Algific game pledging to
ever remain then from north south west
and east came now bellowing/slobbering
unbridled slouching/lumbering wildly
quavers the treacherous beast and...

Alas, Alas grasps/clings here/fear that
draws/near the final days have begun

Words Can Wait

Ahhh, now there you are
I thought you would never
get here
I have been waiting oh
such a long while
Waiting for you to come
along and charge my life
The shadows of waiting
are dark as dark
They create a perfect
world of wonder
Wonder if someone will
come read
wonder if I am really
something to read
Maybe I'm just a half
thought idea left to
grow into full measure
wandering still in a void
of is or maybe not
Then I feel you take me
I feel you lift me up
Yes, yes, read me, read
me

complete me, be the
culmination of the idea
For my existence is only
truly completed when you
read me

No, no don't stop, don't
put me down
Don't lay me back away in
the shadows of the shelves
Don't, don't...
Okay, okay maybe some other
time
Maybe tomorrow I'll peak
your interest
I'll be here waiting
It is the one thing these
marks you see on the
support before your eyes
do innately
It is the essence of
their very nature

How long will I wait
An hour, days, months,
years
Oh I wait...
Infinity upon infinity
It is the bit in life that

Exposing Myself

I do best
I know this without even
reading myself
What I am made of is
timeless
It is my truest virtue for

Words can wait Forever

Write Write Write

*One reason I don't suffer Writer's Block is that I
don't wait on the muse, I summon it at need. - Piers
Anthony*

*Write, write, write
through the day and
into the night, don't
wait for new fuel
just get up and take
flight, don't
attempt to be wrong or
even to be right just
plug into yourself and
enter the light for
deep inside lays untapped
insight and out of this
dark comes ideas bright
that carries us kites on
highs beyond height and
strength beyond might
enveloped in vision
beyond sight so*

Write, write, write

Part IV: Somewhere Near Love

Stanley Christopher

In Those Eyes

He looked into those eyes. Somehow he knew those eyes. He saw himself in those glistening orbs. Not his reflection, but something. Something like, like, his... soul?

And As I Prepare To Leave

And as I prepare to leave
I gather all the misty memories like
gossamer twine, to accompany the
loneliness and pain of the portion
of freedom that beckons
I brush my face lightly against yours
and flutter inside with tingles of
joy and wonder at how you
still electrify me though the flame
flickers and ebbs, so shallow
For inside it tickles the chorus
of distant lose and is
at once bitter/sweet

And as I prepare to leave
I sort out all the particulars like
inventoried stock in a passion shop
to befriend the unsparing twinges
of hurt and sadness, Like pieces,
your fat hairy sex the, detachments
of your orgasms the, feel of your skin
when something makes your flesh crawl
So many distractions alienating in
their mellifluous smoothcitingness
at once candied hemlock

Exposing Myself

And as I prepare to leave
I drink in at the springs of nectar
that has pulsed elixir,
that gave breath unto this
prison shrouded with doubt
and distrust, in empty hopes
and attempts at belief
I partook of the tainted fruit
and gagged on the vomit it
forced me to wallow in and it was
at once the image of you

Alas...
Sometimes the bad truly does
outweigh the good

Billie

She pursued me aggressively
I wasn't that difficult to
catch
I took her home with me that
first night
And for five years we were
together

She showed me she loved me
openly
Turned her back each night
reaching back
She chain smoked in fear of
loosing me
I hated it out loud and said
so often

Last time I saw her
skin
had paled
The rosy red had seeped to
dark circles
The sickness was consuming
her beautiful
My wish cancer will someday
devour itself

Caught Forever

And here in the midst

of waiting

relating to the

anticipation

I find your soul

stationed

And I primal beast

of ever was

devour every

morsel of your

tender love

Insatiable is my

appetite

Endless is the

shear delight

Stanley Christopher

Resplendent in the

grasp of light

caught forever

in the ether

of anticipation

Damn I Can Hardly Wait

You know it just hit me again...
Damn I can hardly wait to see you...
to have you in the same room with me...
to hear your voice on me...
to taste your scent in my head...
to sense your heat...
to smell your speech...
to find how deep inside you reach...
Damn I can hardly wait to see you...
You know it just hit me again...

Do You Even Know

What is this meandering
dance about
What's all this twisting,
turning, in and out
Thought my vision was
clear now I'm in doubt
I went one way you took
an altered route

Your confusion also has
me confused
All the soft innocent
language you used
Already feel that I'm
being abused
This is real messed up
however it's viewed

Made it clear I was
getting into you
You could have been straight
when this was brand new
Instead you let me court
you, not a clue
And you baited 'til the
attraction grew

Exposing Myself

You let me go on, never
said a word
Just interested in the
song you heard
Didn't care in the end
I'd feel absurd
What selfishness on your
part has occurred

Do you even know you've
toyed with my heart
Dined on my emotions
like ale' cart
Now you feign innocence
like you had no part
Let me place the horse
back before the cart

This is the shame and
this is on the ground
When love streams in it's
hard to turn around
Because of this, right
now my heart is bound
But you'll never savor
this new love found

Stanley Christopher

'Til the end of time this
question remains
Will the loss of this love
outweigh your gains
I pray you end up with no
sad refrains
I'm blessed we brushed souls
it was worth all the pains

Electric Eclectic Love

Pouring molten hot golden slot
ebony seas beholding razor edged
breezes sheering lust saturated
creases through valleys pulsing
endearing careening adhering
sticky slick honeysuckle licked
dripping space lingering taste
warm orgasmic laced tunnel and
pooling place lapping throbbing
walls strawberry licorice soaked
halls panting smoldering stoked
searing rear entry enduring to
levels curing impossible desires
igniting perpetual fires drenched
in ecstasy divinely celestial
recipes climbing counting endlessly
mounting slipping sliding dipping
colliding exhausting wet coming to
rest in the calm of the crest that
is how it works the sparks are set
until it blows out a spent circuit

For The Sake Of Being Us

I thought of you as I
made love to her last night
And a hunger denied is
building within my chest
But you came/went like a
ghost on the wispy evening
breeze of a burning grey dawn
And my spirit misses the
heated flame you nurtured in
the churning soil of your
assonant bosom, jet crimson
with the re-spurned life of
a million fires, left for dead

I searched the twilight skies
for your presence and found
only whispers far at the edge
of sound like metal flakes
drifting up the canyons of your
memory, paled and faded but
never finished, as the story
lingers once again to a screeching
pause of ambered hesitation,
balanced upon the slow precipice

Exposing Myself

of your desire and I stand
granite in the waxy clouds
awaiting your moistened decent

I Be Hers And

I be hers and
she be mine but
she just don't
want me all the
time
but when she do
it's oh so good
heaven on earth
I knock on wood
oh but I love
her so I'm still
kind because she
forever be on my
mind
so I will be
with her when I
can because she
my woman and I
be her man

It's You That I Miss

I miss whispering sweet
tender words in your ears
The ones that I spoke from
the heart, revealing fears
The ones that would bring
subside to all your tears
The ones that assured I'd
be there through the years

I can feel the crushing
distance as we grow apart
A most unbearable thing I
couldn't dream would start
One of those things like
acid rain eating my heart
leaving me sitting in love
like a broken down cart

So I found myself clutching
dreams that can't come true
The thinness of this hope
leaving me feeling dry blue
Because somewhere down deep
inside I guess that I knew
The light that I wanted is
not the love that we grew

Stanley Christopher

So I find myself lost in the mist
Filled with this absence of bliss
Overwhelmed by love I can't resist
Rooted in, "it's you that I miss"

Memories of You

I've put my memories of you
in a box with all my dead
And no one will recognize you
because I removed the head

Poem One

on average I would have
liked you
but you are more than
average
deeper than average
And your beauty your
intelligence
swallowed me like
Jonah leaving
me to
search you inside
attempting to
find where I
belonged seeking to
know if the music
pouring from your
pen bleeding my heart
was sacred or the
belly of a whale or
a wistful basket of
poisonous ivy
irritating my throat
as I inhale your
pulsing parameters
and drown in your
golden red sands

Revealing Selves (A Sonnet)

Why do you reveal all yourselves to me
So many secret selves laid out to see
Hidden from view with false integrity
Yet brought lighted for me open and free

What do I do that relaxes you so
That you offer yourself from head to toe
and pretend to yourself that I don't know
the depths of the darkness that lurks below

Guess everyone needs someone just like me
No preconceived notions that you should be
Supporting your growth to its full degree
Not doubting in judgment, a fair referee

We know one day I'll be gone, it's true
And then who will you reveal yourselves to

Shook Her Hard

Shook her with my eyes
hooked her with my mouth
looked her into my skies
from her north to south

Held her up to my light
tasted her to my through
held her down into bright
sniffed her glittered dew

Stroked her neck savory
coated fingers sliding by
breathing caramel bravery
scented stiff of dragonfly

Sirens

*Rakes - Insatiably adore the opposite sex and their desire is infectious

*Sirens - Aphrodite - have an abundance of sexual energy and know how to use it / *Coquettes, esthetics, charismatics, stars, ideal lovers, dandies, naturals

*Sirens - Represents a powerful seductive male fantasy, highly sexual supremely confident alluring female, offering endless pleasure and a bit of danger. Adventurers, risk takers.

Turn this strong virulent male into your slave
lock me out of your chamber, leave me to rant
and rave and in just the nick of time come along
and save my battered brow and wounded heart for
your kind of energy I crave. Most potent your
unimaginable power so seductive my heart slams
in my chest when you are near. Being the rigid
masculine type, your magic has worked on me well
You have distinguished yourself to me from all
women. You are by nature a prized being. And I
the consummate intellectual, find myself most
susceptible falling under your spell and like
the writer/thinker, Julius Caesar, I have

transfixed my intellectual abilities onto this;
love's battlefield

*You are a mirage, luring, cultivating that certain
appearance
and that steamy manner, emoting my fantasy,
controlling my libido

Smiling Roses (For Mz. Monica)

She's there, I have never heard her voice
But she is there, I see her lovely visage
Her beauty speaks to me, it whispers to me
its' mystery, and I am intrigued, shaken
even, my mind reels, hypnotic eyes blaze
tunnels, mines caverns, spinning, twisting,
slipping through my being, beyond my being
dipping to lick my aching soul, bathes me,
soothing the ugliness of my hunger, senses
coming clear. I know it is as it should be,
she has touched me, spoken soft to my heart
the tenderness of her silent voice, the glow
of her cosmically luscious skin, then comes
the playful question

Are you trying to make me blush?

My heart whispers... yessssss...
As her cheeks flush golden pink...

Smiling Roses

Still Praying

I was as sweet to you as I
knew how to be
I prayed to God to be even
sweeter
But that only left me feeling
like you owed me something
That left me feeling guilty
'cause my Daddy had always
taught me different
He always showed me how
to love differently
To love unconditionally
never expecting any return
But I couldn't feel that
I loved you to hard
It made me want you to
love me back hard
When you didn't love me
back hard
When you walked over my love
It made me love you
with hate
It made me love you with
angry hate

It made me pray to God
to remove you from me
Remove you from my heart
and soul
Because my Daddy taught me
God would rescue
So I prayed my heart be
changed and my soul be
relieved from the pain
I'm still praying night and
day

Sit Me Up in the Pit of Your Arm (A Little Freeform)

Sit me up in the pit of your arm, stick
me up in the pit of your arm
Wish I could fit in the pit of your arm

Nestled tight in the bristled soft nest
in the pit of your arm
All moist and warm permeating my being
with the damp sweaty muskiness of your
juicy Black scent, penetrating needle
pheromones, loading, over-loading,
drenching my senses, impregnating my
cells, my atoms, my protons, my neutrons, my
electrons,
invading my nuclei... each orgasm is a
tiny death
Kill me, kill me and kill me again.

Side Note: Each time a cell in a body dies, it is
replaced at the very same moment by a brand new
cell, the new cell contains all the D.N.A. and other
genetic information that was contained in the
expired cell, plus any new information that may
have been generated during the period of expiration
and new birth. The intelligence in-born in these cells

130

are the reason you knew to suck your thumb as a
baby without ever being taught how to.

Stuff me full of you, pack me beyond capacity
make me obese with you, gorge me with you,
gluttonize me on your onyx latescence, feed
my greed, plant your seed, the essence of why
we breed, feed me, feed me, nurture me,
wet-nurse me, fondle me, nourish me, cultivate,
cherish, cradle me, suckle me, sustain me,
birth me, birth me, create me anew, give me re-
birth,
give me re-birth, give me re-birth, give me...

Sit me up in the pit of your arm, stick
me up in the pit of your arm
Wish I could fit in the pit of your arm

Stanley Christopher

Symptoms of You

I venture into your eyes
and sonatas play Spring
time toning into me butter
flies bellow the scent of
peonies fill full my head
fluttering magnolias couch
my brain dripping winged
beats that sweat like hot
Saturday nights of catfish
and straightening combs
and rest in melodies of
Nina being Simoned feeling
good in jazzy syncopation
marching into bluesy heated
retreat ripe drudging love
quivers hard ball/chained
in a garden of startled
flamingos draping across
fluid skies of pink shadows

Tender Genesis

I.

From smoky shadows freshly
stroked long ago abandoned
to a dusty cornered memory
locked away back there home
the birth life and death of
a pre-pubescent advent soon
spawned awake by clash and
moans that froze young raw
hearts in the strange airs
of night transferred in the
odors of stale pleasantries

II.

Hushed ceremony innocence
pinned down squished buried
in an old coal shed that
lingers in the throes of
slow leaning demise mashed
in on the ancient dried out
juices and fused over used
imaginations parochial day
dreams fueled to life in a

Stanley Christopher

childish void of shared duo
ignorance sustaining first
initial joys and quiet sins
in an urban garden of Eden

The Judgment

I have died inside today
And freedom has returned
Some great yearning has
ceased and passed away

The eon of attrition is
at an end, it is finished
My vision clears rapidly
in this new sprung light

No longer shall I dwell
in that lonely confused
darkness
And you, your hands steel
vises clasped at my neck
ranting and raving of the
risk I took for freedom

You hold me fettered and
chained eternally in the
wickedness of your cruel
unspoken promises and
lies, You are one of the
cardinal effects I must
put away. New day, and
you, living obstruction,
impede increase.

Stanley Christopher

Arresting the rise and
the flight of the soul
Phoenix, rebirth. So the
ultimate sacrifice is
the judgment, my love.

For you no longer deserve
my unconditional focus

The Only Light

Sometimes you pray for
a song to sing and find
you have no voice
Sometimes you must put
things away because you
have no choice

Sometimes you must
endure the pain that is
ripping you apart
And on your knees deep
in the night pray GOD
just steel your heart

Sometimes you can not
run away from what is
churning inside of you
Sometimes heartbreak
like lost madness burns
you through and through

Sometimes as the saying
goes it can last only for
a season
Sometimes when done is
done we're blessed to
know the reason

Stanley Christopher

Sometimes we're blinded
by the scorching love that
truly deeply binds
And forget lost in our
darkness
it's the only light
that shines

To Mine Self Be True

You are concerned
that I'm in love
with you
and upset when you
feel me backing out
If I let it slide
this would mix me up
or is that what
this is all about

It's like some kind
of mental Kung Fu
that leaves me on
the cold bloody ground
And as much as I think
of you I guess I'm
finally coming around

This is something you
can't commit to but as
yet you won't let go
You planted a seed that
rooted true and grew
And now you must reap
what you sow

And as uncomfortable as
this feels to me
I know it is what I
must do
It's the only way that
I can see
To mine self to be true

Tragedy of Love

I looked for you in the rain
between the drops in the dry
Drew you deep into my sane
as my madness sought to fly
I supped on you through my drain
and your wanting made me cry
I chewed upon your neat complain
and your brain just made me sigh
All this love thing is in vain
and I'm pleased to tell you why
tragedy's always laced with pain
bound with ribbons in the sky

Twas Better

There's no way to save some
things we deem precious
No matter how deeply these
things may touch us
Sometimes we just don't have
any choice
And our desires are trapped
by silent voice
So all that is left is for
us to carry on
While praying the searing
pain soon be gone
And know in our hearts that
we will
Swallow hard and get past
this bitter pill
And in the end hear the
heavens call
Twas better to love and loose
than not love at all

Way Past The Time

You are right
I need someone
who is present
who is here
and not someone
so distant that
they never feel
near

So far remote
so far removed
a great excuse
why love can
never be proved

Now at this point
I know that I must
reap what I sow
for it is way past
the time
for me to let go

What is it That Flows in You

What is it that flows in you
grows in you, imbuing you,
renewing you
that makes your libido scream
like that, a heated cat,
clawing at your inner
thermostat, blowing you
full of holes, burning you
like steaming coals
wringing your body out
draining your fired spout
dripping and oozing wet
releasing the flames
without regret
quenching of your hungry
thirst, reaching nirvana
'bout to burst

What is it that flows in you

Wounded Un-Wounded

In the beginning she was always there
mollycoddling, stroking, hugging, encroaching
Every bit of her exuding all consuming love
Feminism brought her more gender power
an overwhelming power that crushed his
masculine, made him seek out to the
feminine as key to his salvation looking for
her surrogate in a world of female orchestrate

Consumed by industry and a continuous need to
provide, he was there yet separate in a way
A father in a self-induced industrial exile
Never the capacity to deliver the sacred wound
that he never received from his father
Never taking the sacred journey, he could never
teach his son to walk the walk of sacred king

Working and resting only to work some more
No leisure time, no true family time, resented
for not being there, available, the separation
a healed over scab covering a festering, growing
blooming wound underneath

The equality of King and Queen goes missing, lost
His inner god self-consumed by goddess, his true

sacred inner king suppressed, over-sensitive,
repressed the clinging to goddess grew and was
transferred to an immature society cursed by a
shallow immature view, further complicated by the
absence of a true king, the world withdrew
grieving, leaving it to a new Shadow Warrior

A warrior who never learned the lesson of the
sacred wound that separated and joined King with
Queen, spirit with nature, youthful man to god-head
A center stunted in growth, leaving only the
budding of a man, inadequate prince becomes
inadequate king, unable to recognize the divine
within self an under developed sense of sacred

purpose and power, robbed of his true birthright

Part V: Your Cup Of Joe Before Bed

#1 Through #25

Stanley Christopher

#1

The wistful foggy
thoughts of dawn
fade lost into the day
We drink our coffee
in the morn
daring feats of clay
Poets throw loose
words around that
land in disarray
At night we lay our
bodies down and to
Dear God we pray

#2

Into the void mine
heart is drawn
approaching all in
faith
In that space love
new to spawned
I trust believe
and wait

For in this place my
inner truth's loosed
away from hate
fills up my gratitude
for the treasures put
on my plate

#3

Intrinsic notes echo
clear announcing into
night
Essential rests hours
dear reflecting loves
delight
Magical drifts voices
cheer foretelling our
height
up surging souls arise
near ascending unto
flight

#4

Her slickness belies my
trust as the lies turn
to dust in my eyes and
my cringing heart hides
in fear of being spied
inside a weak shell it
cries at the notion of
lost and found and so
sighs with no place in
which to safely reside

#5

Cherry blossoms and
lions teeth lay up
underneath a spell of
disbelief soaked in
the juice of a leaf
fallen from the tree
that bears the grief
of distant sorrow
and little relief in
a tomorrow forecasted
for needed peace yet
it all relies upon
what we all believe

#6

Unicorns with twisted
horns are fantasies I
can't afford
I live a life cast of
varied storms seeking
due accord
filigree and candied
corn melt away at dawn
new adored
pearlescent words rosy
thorns bare my fleshly
blood poured

#7

Even as I consume the
feeding of your fire
I pant with raw desire
in a need to acquire
the magic feel of your
weight pressing

wait

undressing my fate in
that place upon my
face that sumptuous hot
plate feeding my urge
to relate...

okay that's enough...

for some reason I
feel I need an ice
cold shower

#8

Endless thirsty my desire

The essence of your Nubia

The radiant light of your dark

The portrayal of your raven

The twisted jet of your spark

The slick slipping of your onyx

The inky rhythm of your pitch

The cool patience of your ebony

The sucking soul of your eclipse

The sooty still of your shadow

The redbone of your obsidian

The sensuous of your starless

The undertaking of your black

You are an oasis along my journey

#9

Be About Love

Be about love
be endearing
and gentle be
nurturing and
kind keeping
in mind and
also in heart
this the cause
of your birth

Be about love

#10

peer tele
scope
mind sweep
deep
down
steep
com
plete
into my
bottomless
s
l
e
e
p

twist
my
heart 'til
my
black
drips
oily
over your

158

Exposing Myself

jeweled
dew
primed
butter
fly
wings

sharpen
taut
your cup
cakes
awake
un
bend
ing
upon
my
savored
thoughts

dip me
under
neath
slip
me
through
up and
over
into

Stanley Christopher

the soft
funnel
re
c
e
i
v
i
n
g
me

you

160

#11

The sound of
your
voice still
lights the
heart
As in the
begin where
it first
came to
start
centering
in on
the
target a
spiritual
dart
adhering
in
permanence
ne'er
to depart

#12

Her in golden coffee
Him home in white T
Soft sigh at black lace
taste testing to face
the distance so long
the miss tense a song
enveloped smooth heat
wash rinse and repeat

#13

Are you trying
to figure if
I am still
lost do
I need
you
to save
me
rescue
me

the answers
come
daily
and you
have
be come
my
soul's
on going
work
in
progress

#14

You linger stormy
about my shoulders
my chest roars out
your name framed in
the rattle of your
taut thighs sighs
gasping for breath
as art that parts to
single winged flight
in ecstasy wrapped
in soft graces and
multifaceted paces
of thundered rhythm
mixed into rhyme in
moist metered time
winding around upon
freedom rides glide
you to linger stormy
about my shoulders
and again my chest
roars out your name

my chest roars out
your name

#15

I want to behold
your heart wrap
it together unto
mine in a banding
of impenetrable
love as a flexible
steel wall of razor
barbed wire to sway
and swing and to be
spiritual metronome
warmly ticking away
the measure of lost
and found embraces
to the peeling of
tiny bells of time
shifting the sands
of the hour glasses
of our own lives

#16

Survivor's Prayer

I cannot undo the
pains I've endured
but assuredly I can
celebrate coming on
through the flames
the flying through
the parting of the
smoke and pushed in
my prevailing into
survival I scream

burn me!! burn me!!
then burn me again!!!

#17

Ever been alone...
in a quiet place...
a special place...
drifting to love...
with the words of...
the raw spirit of...
one special other...
Ever had your soul
peeled open... mmmm

#18

When I am lonely for a girl,
it's not really the girl I'm
missing, not in her totality
anyway. It's the curl of her
inner thigh, the moistness
of her sex, the slope of her
lower back just at her waist.
The scent of her, fresh from
the shower; the raw heat of
her at the climax of one of
her prolonged orgasms. The
sway of her breasts as she
walks naked across a room.
The salty crease where her
neck and shoulder meet. The
fuzzy careen from naval to
Venus' mount and the coarse
spiritual silence when our
eternal souls are entwined.

#19

From the beginning
I wondered if ever
you would love me

Oh I know you do
but oh if you did
the way that I want
you too

come to me be with
me because you can
not see any other
way to be

attached deep onto
me at a cellular
level sweet tender
super glued mellow

All caught up fast
beyond I'm just here
decided to be with
you 'cause I need to

be caught up into
nowhere else even
spiritually freely
locked into me

From the beginning
I wondered if ever
you could true be
into love with me

#20

I unaware from whence
it came with the quiet
of a hush it came with
a voice, a voice with
the distain of a woman
it came roaring with
the pitifulness of a
man, it entered inside
consuming me speaking
out of captured mouth
peeling through lips
bells clanging into an
injured soul spilling
spewing a cackling sea
flooding of superlatives
comparatives positives
negatives cashing in on
vast voids of emptiness
and I howled into the
night of my desperation
envy grasped upon my
heart releasing every
concern as I summoned
to testify before the

Stanley Christopher

court of mankind hence
to throw my omnificent
pleas at the strained
mercies of all womanhood

#21

You came into my
dreams last night
Perfectly you
stood by my side
Ride or die?
You came to ride
Didn't have to
question or fight
Your actions to
me made you right
Deep down I knew
I could confide
It's you for me
It can't be denied

#22

I wonder what your
aroma tastes like
I ponder on your
love full unbound
in endless flight
Will your words
feel like sage
lavender and lace
As my heart plants
light loving kisses
all over your face
We should build an
alliance that will
endure through all
time stable and
strong resting in
a quality of prime
I beckon you dear
heart this be true
worthy to be tried
we can stay here as
one together to be
continued in time
on the next side

#23

Broken

To catch this sudden wave of you
Makes me cry with pain
As I continue my journey
Without you
Keeping Shredded
Heart close
As it clings to Life
Wanting to Die
But will not

Every day, I will wait
'til you're mine again
I will die everyday
'til you're mine again
brings me close to the day
when you're mine again
there's no words to explain
no beginning and no end
I will dream, I will pray
you'll be mine again

#24

Hearing your voice again
made my heart spin and
my brain blend thoughts
and memories of the good
without the bad me on my
knees as I determined to
please you on your back
thighs locked on squeeze
whispering my name afraid
to release lost in that warm
raw space of trying not to
breath finally letting go
a ruptured dam flooding
the valley with can't hold
any longer floating upon
a river of lust satisfied
feeding that hunger inside
that would not be denied

#25 (For Mz. Tajuana)

Something about a woman
with moles on her face
An old school charm with
a simple kind of grace
Small beauty marks that
dapple 'cross her cheeks
a mystery whispering of
what a real man seeks
Promises of splendor and
soft clouds full of dreams
No need for shadowy
make-up or exotic creams
And nothing in Nature
could ever replace that
something about a woman
with moles on her face

Made in the USA
Charleston, SC
26 January 2015